The CANVAS of TOMORROW

Nehemiah and the story of one church in a challenged neighborhood

STUDY GUIDE

Copyright © 2021 by Bishop J. W. Macklin

Published by AVAIL

All rights reserved. No portion of this book may be reproduced, stored in a retrieval system, or transmitted in any form or by any means—electronic, mechanical, photocopy, recording, scanning, or other—except for brief quotations in critical reviews or articles, without prior written permission of the author.

Scripture quotations marked KJV are taken from the King James Version of the Bible. | Scripture quotations marked NKJV are taken from the New King James Version®. Copyright © 1982 by Thomas Nelson. Used by permission. All rights reserved.

For foreign and subsidiary rights, contact the author.

Cover design by: Joe De Leon
Cover Photo by: Andrew van Tilborgh

ISBN: 978-1-954089-75-4   1 2 3 4 5 6 7 8 9 10

Printed in the United States of America

BISHOP J.W. MACKLIN

The
CANVAS *of*
TOMORROW

Nehemiah and the story of
one church in a challenged
neighborhood

STUDY GUIDE

CONTENTS

Chapter 1. We All Have a Canvas 6

Chapter 2. Do You Hear What I Hear? 12

Chapter 3. Tell Me What You Feel 18

Chapter 4. Ministry Is Risky Business 24

Chapter 5. Step Out or Step Back 30

Chapter 6. Seeing Through the Darkness 36

Chapter 7. Fighting Above Your Weight 42

Chapter 8. Doing All to Stand 48

Chapter 9. Good Trouble Ahead 54

Chapter 10. The Stone the Builders Rejected 60

CHAPTER 1

WE ALL HAVE A CANVAS

The canvas on which we paint may be dark or light, clean or smudged, but it's the canvas God has given us to paint a masterpiece.

As you read Chapter 1: "We All Have a Canvas" in *The Canvas of Tomorrow*, review, reflect on, and respond to the text by answering the following questions.

REVIEW, REFLECT, AND RESPOND:

In general, how do you deal with change?

_____
_____
_____
_____
_____
_____
_____
_____
_____
_____
_____
_____

In what area of your life are you desperate to see change?

_____
_____
_____
_____
_____
_____
_____
_____
_____

Reflect on Bishop Macklin's theme:

> If your circumstances are going to change, you must take the brush of faith and paint *in vibrant living color on the canvas of your tomorrow.*

What canvas has God given you?

_____
_____
_____
_____
_____
_____
_____
_____
_____
_____

What is your vision for your "Canvas of Tomorrow"?

_____
_____
_____
_____
_____
_____
_____
_____
_____
_____

How do you differentiate between a wish, a dream, and a vision?

_____
_____
_____
_____
_____
_____
_____

Re-evaluate your vision for your Canvas of Tomorrow based on Bishop Macklin's statement: "A vision has two parts: the problem and a possible solution." What are your two parts?

The Problem: _____
_____
_____
_____
_____
_____

Possilble Solution: _____
_____
_____
_____
_____
_____

> *Where there is no vision, the people perish*
> —*Proverbs 29:18 (KJV)*

Consider the Scripture and answer the following questions:

What vision do you believe the writer of Proverbs is talking about?

_____
_____
_____
_____
_____
_____

In what way might people perish—figuratively or literally—if you don't pursue the solution part of your vision?

_____
_____
_____
_____
_____
_____

Which part of your vision are you going to have to depend on God or other people to fulfill?

_____
_____
_____
_____

What resistance are you expecting to face as you attempt to fulfill your vision?

___

Who can rally around you like the immediate and extended community rallied around Bishop Macklin when his life was threatened?

___

What do you need to do to enlist that help?

___

CHAPTER 2

DO YOU HEAR WHAT I HEAR?

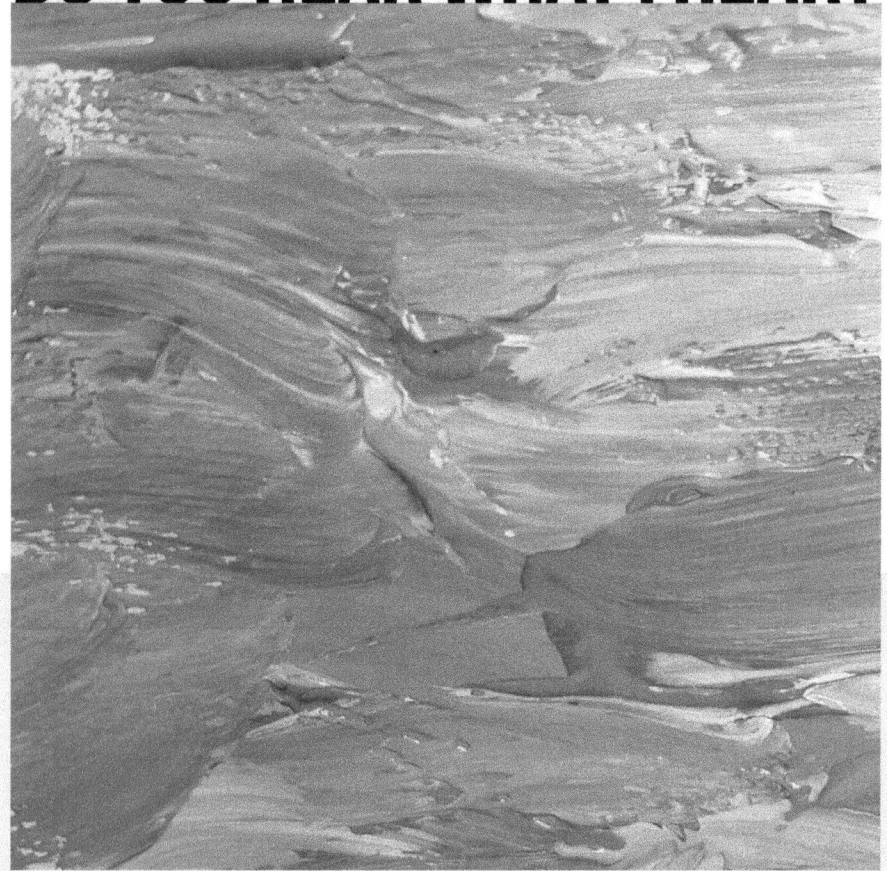

We may think prophets and other extraordinary people are the only ones who can hear God's voice, but that's not true at all.

As you read Chapter 2: "Do You Hear What I Hear?" in *The Canvas of Tomorrow*, review, reflect on, and respond to the text by answering the following questions.

REVIEW, REFLECT, AND RESPOND:

What is your experience with God "talking" to people?

_____
_____
_____
_____
_____
_____
_____
_____
_____
_____
_____
_____

In your opinion, how *does* God speak to people in the 21st century?

_____
_____
_____
_____
_____
_____
_____
_____
_____
_____
_____
_____

What role does the Holy Spirit play in your life?

_____
_____
_____
_____
_____
_____
_____
_____

How would you know if the Holy Spirit were directing you to change course or direction?

_____
_____
_____
_____
_____
_____
_____
_____

How do you know when you're listening?

_____
_____
_____
_____
_____

What challenges do you think Nehemiah faced when Hanani and his friends brought the message about Jerusalem and the brothers and sisters there?

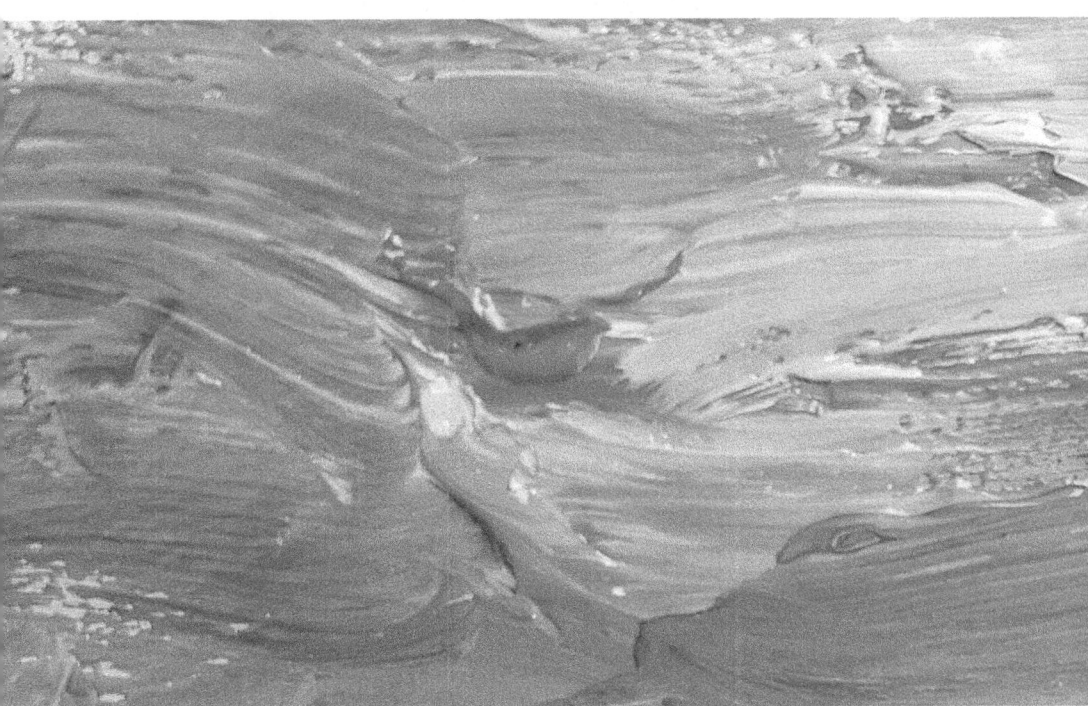

> *Though the Lord gives you*
> *The bread of adversity and the water of affliction,*
> *Yet your teachers will not be moved into a corner anymore,*
> *But your eyes shall see your teachers.*
> *Your ears shall hear a word behind you, saying,*
> *"This is the way, walk in it,"*
> *Whenever you turn to the right hand*
> *Or whenever you turn to the left.*
>
> —Isaiah 30:20-21 (NKJV)

Consider the Scripture and answer the following questions:

What adversity do people face when they're trying to follow God's will?

_____
_____
_____
_____
_____

What comfort can you take from Isaiah's words?

_____
_____
_____
_____
_____

What can people trust if they are listening for God's voice?

_____
_____
_____
_____
_____

What have you asked God for that is going to require you to listen carefully?

_____
_____
_____
_____

What is God speaking to you regarding what you're painting on your canvas?

_____
_____
_____
_____

What steps can you take to sharpen your hearing and clear your thoughts, so you can heed God's voice and obey?

_____
_____
_____
_____

What do you think the consequences of your obedience are going to be?

_____
_____
_____
_____

CHAPTER 3

TELL ME WHAT YOU FEEL

Powerful feelings of compassion for those who are hurting are the fuel of good and godly activism, whether the hurting people are under our roofs, live down the street, or are on the other side of town. They're all infinitely valuable to God.

As you read Chapter 3: "Tell Me What You Feel" in *The Canvas of Tomorrow*, review, reflect on, and respond to the text by answering the following questions.

REVIEW, REFLECT, AND RESPOND:

In general, what is your attitude toward feelings?

_____
_____
_____
_____
_____
_____
_____
_____
_____
_____

What prevents you from experiencing deep affection for God?

_____
_____
_____
_____
_____
_____
_____
_____
_____
_____

When was the last time you felt the burden of grief on behalf of God and His kingdom?

_____
_____
_____
_____
_____
_____
_____
_____

What was your response to that grief?

_____
_____
_____
_____
_____
_____
_____
_____

Respond to Bishop Macklin's pronouncement: "It is my deep belief that you must feel something before you see something."

_____
_____
_____

What about our modern existence might prevent us from feeling as acutely as we could? How might that affect our "seeing"?

> *Therefore it is of faith that it might be according to grace, so that the promise might be sure to all the seed, not only to those who are of the law, but also to those who are of the faith of Abraham, who is the father of us all (as it is written, "I have made you a father of many nations") in the presence of Him whom he believed—God, who gives life to the dead and calls those things which do not exist as though they did; who, contrary to hope, in hope believed, so that he became the father of many nations, according to what was spoken, "So shall your descendants be."*
>
> —Romans 4:16-18 (NKJV)

Consider the Scripture and answer the following questions:

What was Abraham hoping for according to the verses from Romans?

_____
_____
_____
_____

What role did hope play in Abraham's receiving what God had promised to him?

_____
_____
_____
_____

In what areas of your life have you placed your hope in the promises of God?

_____
_____
_____
_____

How does having hope affect the way we bear our burdens and feelings of disappointment?

_____
_____
_____
_____
_____
_____
_____

How are your emotions—or lack thereof—reflected as you paint on your Canvas of Tomorrow?

_____
_____
_____
_____
_____
_____
_____

Describe the vibrance of the colors you're painting with. How satisfied are you with their hues?

_____
_____
_____
_____
_____

CHAPTER 4

MINISTRY IS RISKY BUSINESS

Comfort zones are very attractive, but they're a desert where visions go to die.

As you read Chapter 4: "Ministry Is Risky Business" in *The Canvas of Tomorrow*, review, reflect on, and respond to the text by answering the following questions.

REVIEW, REFLECT, AND RESPOND:

In what ways do you consider yourself responsible?

_____
_____
_____
_____
_____
_____
_____
_____
_____
_____

How do your actual responsibilities or sense of responsibility affect your willingness to take risks?

_____
_____
_____
_____
_____
_____
_____
_____
_____
_____

When was the last time you took a risk? What was the outcome?

What do you think Nehemiah risked by showing his feelings regarding the state of Jerusalem?

How much of Nehemiah's risk was because of the culture in which he was living?

How does your culture—family, occupational, or social—affect your attitudes toward taking risks?

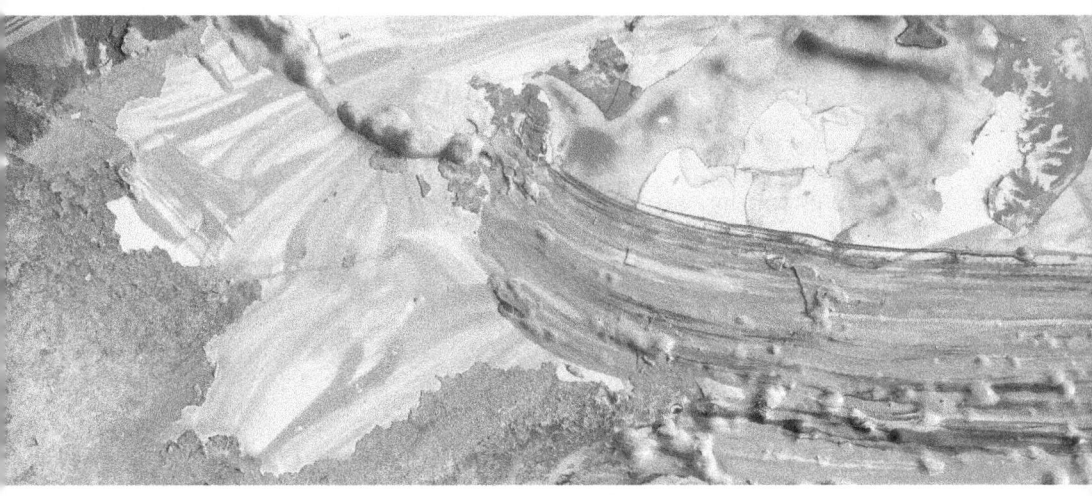

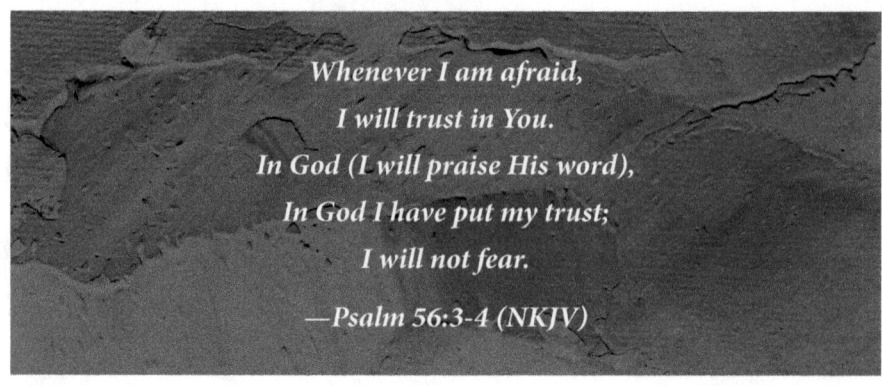

*Whenever I am afraid,
I will trust in You.
In God (I will praise His word),
In God I have put my trust;
I will not fear.*

—Psalm 56:3-4 (NKJV)

Consider the Scripture and answer the following questions:

What causes you—rationally or irrationally—to be afraid?

_____
_____
_____
_____

How do you deal with it?

_____
_____
_____
_____

How do you encourage others who are fearful?

_____
_____
_____
_____

What great accomplishments would never have happened if someone had not left his or her comfort zone and taken a risk?

_____
_____
_____
_____
_____
_____
_____

What is God leading you to paint on your canvas that involves risk?

_____
_____
_____
_____
_____
_____
_____

What's your plan as you anticipate those brushstrokes?

_____
_____
_____
_____
_____
_____
_____

CHAPTER 5

STEP OUT OR STEP BACK

We should never pit faith and action against each other; they are a necessary combination of a Spirit-empowered life.

As you read Chapter 5: "Step Out or Step Back" in *The Canvas of Tomorrow*, review, reflect on, and respond to the text by answering the following questions.

REVIEW, REFLECT, AND RESPOND:

What is your general strategy for decision-making?

_____
_____
_____
_____
_____
_____
_____
_____
_____
_____

Which decisions have been the most momentous in your life so far?

_____
_____
_____
_____
_____
_____
_____
_____
_____
_____

How did you go about deciding what to do?

___

Which part of Bishop Macklin's mantra—Grasp a Vision! Make a Decision! and Move Out!—do you find most challenging? What aspects of that part make it so?

___

What motivates you to press on when you are not confident in either your vision, your decision, or your implementation?

___

_____
_____
_____
_____
_____
_____

How would you encourage someone who is not sure what to do in a given situation, but a choice must be made, and action must be taken?

_____
_____
_____
_____
_____
_____
_____
_____

> *Trust in the Lord with all your heart, And lean not on your own understanding; In all your ways acknowledge Him, And He shall direct your paths.*
>
> *—Proverbs 3:5-6 (NKJV)*

Consider the Scripture and answer the following questions:

When have you had to choose to trust God because your understanding of the situation didn't make sense?

_____
_____
_____
_____
_____
_____

In what ways did you acknowledge Him?

_____
_____
_____
_____
_____
_____

How did He direct your path during this time?

_____
_____
_____
_____
_____

When might the Lord direct a person to move toward darkness?

_____

_____

_____

_____

What do you think Bishop Macklin means when he says, "When we obey and act, we go as far as we can see"? What happens when a person gets that far?

_____

_____

_____

_____

_____

Who inspires you by their ability or willingness to step out in faith and continuing to walk as God reveals further steps?

_____

_____

_____

_____

_____

What is going to happen to the person who insists on seeing the entire "picture" before he or she takes even one step or makes one brushstroke?

_____

_____

_____

_____

CHAPTER 6

SEEING THROUGH THE DARKNESS

Ask God to open your eyes to see great things. By faith, set up your canvas.

As you read Chapter 6: "Seeing Through the Darkness" in The Canvas of Tomorrow, review, reflect on, and respond to the text by answering the following questions.

REVIEW, REFLECT, AND RESPOND:

As you've been working on your Canvas of Tomorrow so far, what moments of awkwardness (similar to 12-year-old Bishop Macklin's suits) have you experienced?

_____
_____
_____
_____
_____
_____
_____
_____
_____

When has it called forth your creativity and tenacity?

_____
_____
_____
_____
_____
_____
_____
_____
_____
_____

THE CANVAS OF TOMORROW: STUDY GUIDE | 37

How has the Master influenced your painting, so it doesn't turn into a "self-portrait"?

___

Bishop Macklin states, "Every genuine movement—spiritual, political, in nonprofit organizations, or in businesses—has two kinds of members: pioneers and settlers." Which one describes you? What causes you to believe that?

___

Why do you think the young pastor who had a vision for 100 members only set up 20 chairs? What value do you see in both men's ideas?

___

In what ways are you a horizontal thinker? In what ways are you a vertical thinker? Which is going to bring you closer to paint in faith on your canvas?

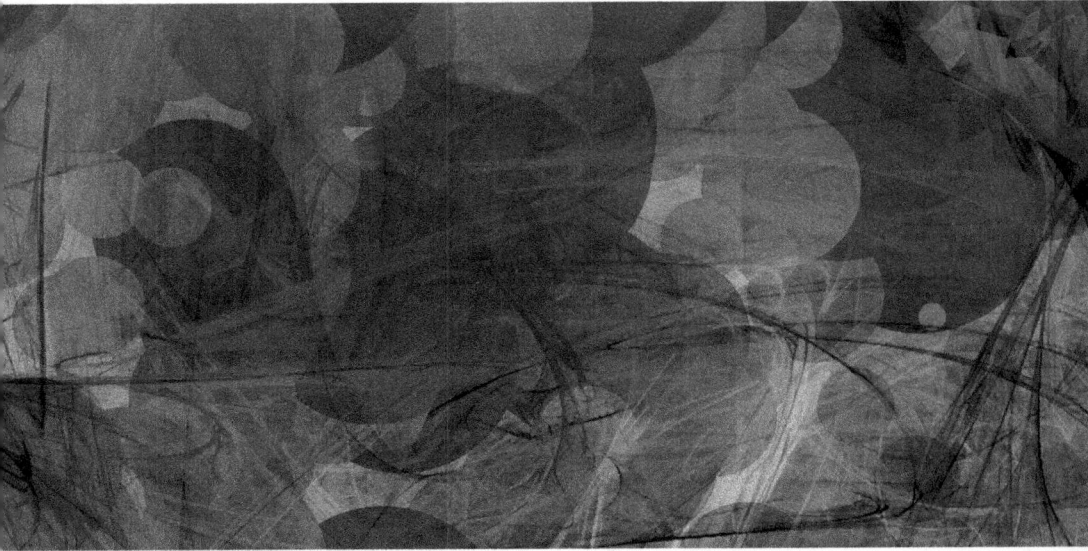

> *But as it is written: "Eye has not seen, nor ear heard, Nor have entered into the heart of man the things which God has prepared for those who love Him." But God has revealed them to us through His Spirit. For the Spirit searches all things, yes, the deep things of God.*
>
> *—1 Corinthians 2:9-10 (NKJV)*

Consider the Scripture and answer the following questions:

What do the verses reveal about things which God has prepared for those who love Him?

_____
_____
_____
_____

Why do those who love God not need to worry about the things God has prepared for them?

_____
_____
_____
_____
_____

What does it mean to you that the Holy Spirit searches the deep things of God?

_____
_____
_____
_____
_____

What tests has life presented for you? How have they gotten increasingly harder?

How can you tell if a test requires "hard" choices or "heart" choices?

How have you seen your faith accumulate with every step you've taken in the "heart" choice decision-making arena?

How has God encouraged you as you've continued to paint on your Canvas of Tomorrow?

CHAPTER 7

FIGHTING ABOVE YOUR WEIGHT

When God uses you to do great things for Him, some will applaud, others will jeer, and still others will run away because miracles make them feel uncomfortable.

As you read Chapter 7: "Fighting Above Your Weight" in *The Canvas of Tomorrow*, review, reflect on, and respond to the text by answering the following questions.

REVIEW, REFLECT, AND RESPOND:

How have you or people you've known experienced, "No great vision goes unopposed"?

What form did that opposition take?

What caused Nehemiah to remain strong in his resolve to rebuild Jerusalem's walls in the face of Sanballat and Tobiah's intimidation tactics?

_____
_____
_____
_____
_____
_____
_____

By the time Bishop Macklin and the church were ready to fashion the abandoned gas station's land into "The Glad Tidings Gateway," what real estate issues had they already surmounted?

_____
_____
_____
_____
_____
_____
_____

How could those issues and solutions have strengthened Glad Tidings' resolve to see God continue to be faithful?

_____
_____
_____
_____
_____

When you face stress and opposition, are you most likely to flee, fight, or freeze? How could each of those responses be transformed constructively?

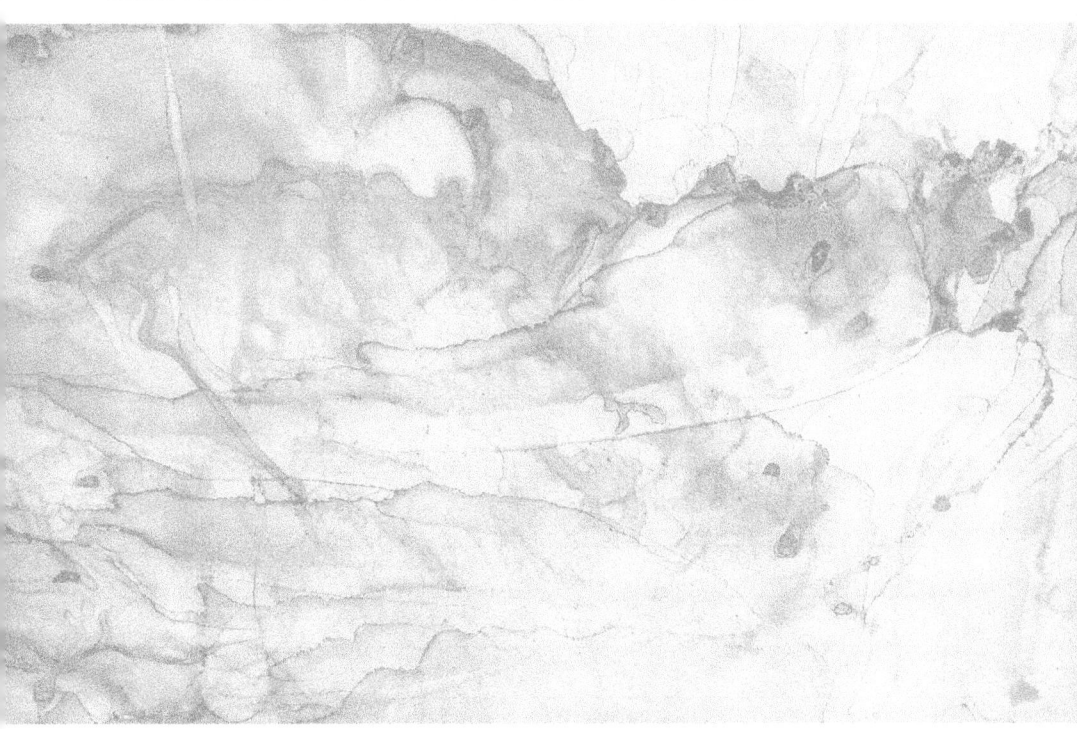

> Yea, though I walk through the valley of the shadow of death,
> I will fear no evil;
> For You are with me;
> Your rod and Your staff, they comfort me.
> —Psalm 23:4 (NKJV)

Consider the Scripture and answer the following questions:

What do you think the psalmist meant when he spoke of the "valley of the shadow of death"?

_____
_____
_____
_____
_____

What does that mean to you?

_____
_____
_____
_____
_____

The Shepherd's rod and staff comfort the psalmist. What comforts you?

_____
_____
_____
_____
_____

In which rings are your brothers and sisters fighting above their weight?

_____
_____
_____
_____
_____
_____

What walls need to be built or torn down, so you can strengthen each other in times of trouble?

_____
_____
_____
_____
_____
_____

What are your next action steps to get that process started?

_____
_____
_____
_____
_____
_____

CHAPTER 8

DOING ALL TO STAND

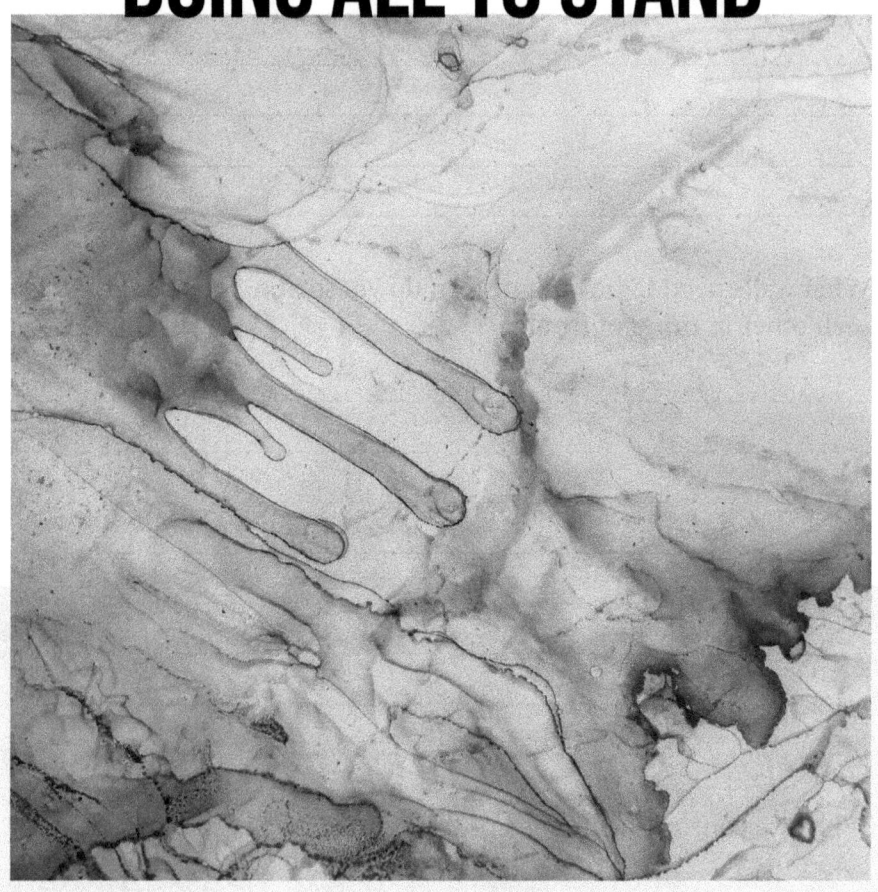

We can throw up our hands and complain that there's nothing we can do about it, or we can do the hard work of identifying the dark powers and taking action to remedy injustice wherever we find it.

As you read Chapter 8: "Doing All to Stand" in *The Canvas of Tomorrow*, review, reflect on, and respond to the text by answering the following questions.

REVIEW, REFLECT, AND RESPOND:

How can you tell your friends from your enemies?

_____
_____
_____
_____
_____
_____
_____
_____
_____
_____

When have you been taken by surprise in this area?

_____
_____
_____
_____
_____
_____
_____
_____
_____
_____

What situations have you faced where the enemy was more than a person? Was it a social construct, political entity, or legislative initiative?

_____
_____
_____
_____
_____
_____
_____
_____

How did or do the people oppressed by the enemy exhibit "learned helplessness"?

_____
_____
_____
_____
_____
_____
_____
_____

How did or do the bystanders also exhibit "learned helplessness"?

_____
_____
_____
_____

Whom do you admire who has found creative solutions to his or her flawed system?

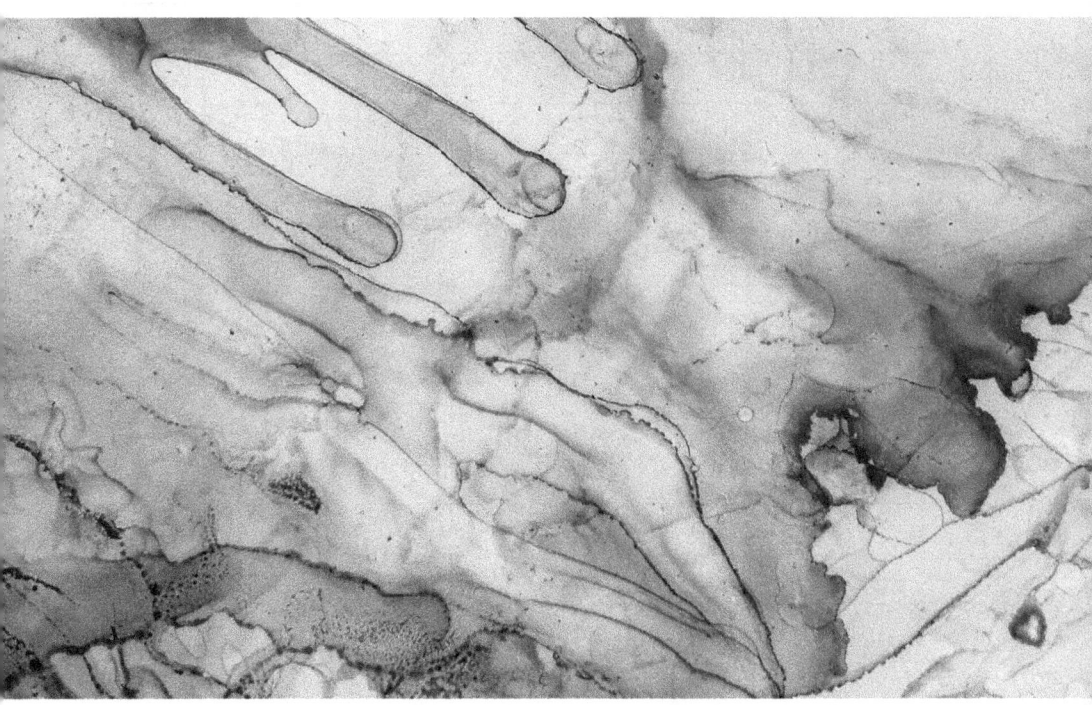

> For I am persuaded that neither death nor life, nor angels nor principalities nor powers, nor things present nor things to come, nor height nor depth, nor any other created thing, shall be able to separate us from the love of God which is in Christ Jesus our Lord.
>
> —Romans 8:38-39 (NKJV)

Consider the Scripture and answer the following questions:

How firmly do you believe Paul's encouragement to the Romans?

_____

_____

_____

_____

_____

_____

_____

_____

_____

Which of the forces that he lists causes you the most concern? Why?

_____

_____

_____

_____

_____

_____

_____

_____

_____

Bishop Macklin states, "We can throw up our hands and complain that there's nothing we can do about it, or we can do the hard work of identifying the dark powers and taking action to remedy injustice wherever we find it." Which of those options has been your traditional method of dealing with injustice?

_____

_____

_____

_____

_____

_____

_____

What can you do now and in the future to be a voice for the voiceless and a lifter of others' heads?

_____

_____

_____

_____

_____

_____

_____

CHAPTER 9

GOOD TROUBLE AHEAD

*It makes no difference who gets the credit
as long as God gets the glory.*

As you read Chapter 9: "Good Trouble Ahead" in *The Canvas of Tomorrow*, review, reflect on, and respond to the text by answering the following questions.

REVIEW, REFLECT, AND RESPOND:

Does the way Nehemiah took control of the situation in Jerusalem inspire you or discourage you? Explain.

_____
_____
_____
_____
_____
_____
_____
_____
_____
_____

In what ways—emotional investment, holy vision, divine faithfulness, and detailed planning—does the method you are following to paint your canvas resemble Nehemiah's method?

_____
_____
_____
_____
_____
_____
_____
_____
_____

Where did Nehemiah meet the last pocket of resistance to rebuilding Jerusalem's walls? How did he deal with it?

_____
_____
_____
_____
_____
_____
_____

How are organization and endurance related?

_____
_____
_____
_____
_____
_____
_____

How did Nehemiah's strength in both areas influence how he interacted with both his supporters and detractors?

_____
_____
_____
_____

_____

_____

_____

_____

In what ways were the workers able to put their personal self-interests aside for the greater good of the nation?

_____

_____

_____

_____

_____

_____

_____

> *Let nothing be done through selfish ambition or conceit, but in lowliness of mind let each esteem others better than himself. Let each of you look out not only for his own interests, but also for the interests of others.*
>
> —Philippians 2:3-4 (NKJV)

Consider the Scripture and answer the following questions:

How hard is it for you to put others' interests above your own?

_____
_____
_____
_____
_____

What role does personality play in a person's ability to follow Paul's instructions?

_____
_____
_____
_____
_____

What hope does a person who struggles to esteem others higher than him or herself have?

_____
_____
_____
_____
_____

Bishop Macklin's congregation joined him in a Jericho-esque march around their neighborhood. In what creative endeavors have you participated or seen others share that represent their cause?

_____
_____
_____
_____
_____
_____
_____

How did those efforts impact their cause? How did they impact the participants' relationships?

_____
_____
_____
_____
_____
_____
_____

What organizations are attempting to paint their Canvases of Tomorrow with vibrant living colors similar to yours? How can you partner with them to further your mutual vision?

_____
_____
_____
_____
_____
_____
_____

CHAPTER 10

THE STONE THE BUILDERS REJECTED

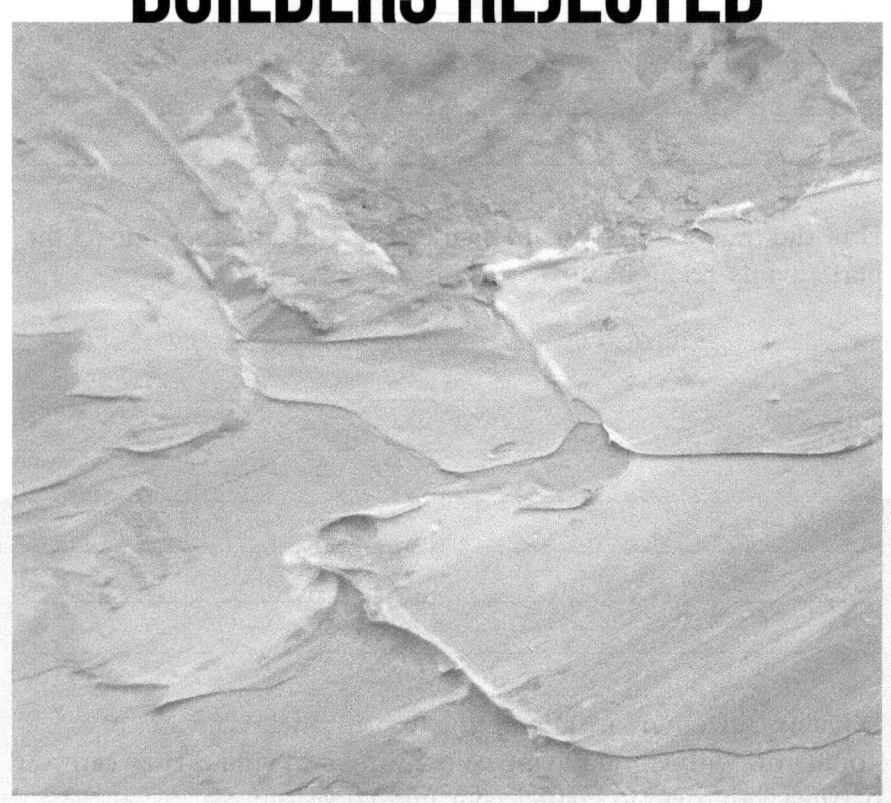

We want to minister to the whole person, not just get them a ticket to heaven when they die. Jesus is King. . . . And God delights in blessing those who call Him Father and Lord.

As you read Chapter 10: "The Stone the Builders Rejected" in *The Canvas of Tomorrow*, review, reflect on, and respond to the text by answering the following questions.

REVIEW, REFLECT, AND RESPOND:

From the moment Nehemiah heard Hanani's news in chapter 1 until Ezra read the Scriptures in chapter 8, how is the way that Nehemiah went about his work of rebuilding the wall different from the way many leaders work today?

_____
_____
_____
_____
_____
_____
_____
_____

Nehemiah heard the news:

_____
_____
_____
_____
_____
_____
_____
_____

Nehemiah talked to King Artaxerxes:

_____
_____
_____
_____
_____
_____

Nehemiah viewed the wall:

_____
_____
_____
_____
_____
_____

Work was started:

_____
_____
_____
_____
_____
_____

Sanballat and Tobiah interfered:

_____
_____
_____

Jewish elite oppressed the workers:

The work was finished:

Ezra read the Law:

> *And whatever you do, do it heartily, as to the Lord and not to men, knowing that from the Lord you will receive the reward of the inheritance; for you serve the Lord Christ.*
>
> —Colossians 3:23-24 (NKJV)

Consider the Scripture and answer the following questions:

How might the verses transform a person's motivation for making a difference in his or her world?

_____
_____
_____
_____
_____

Who is going to benefit from adopting this work ethic?

_____
_____
_____
_____
_____

How does working "as to the Lord" benefit people in the here and now as well as in the future?

_____
_____
_____
_____
_____

Which part of Nehemiah's story has impacted you most deeply?

_____
_____
_____
_____
_____
_____

How has the way he lead the Israelites influence how you live with and lead the people in your family, workplace, school, church, or community?

_____
_____
_____
_____
_____
_____

Bishop Macklin's final words to his readers are these:

Go ahead now, right where you are, close your eyes and see tomorrow with fresh eyes. See God turning it around . . . see change coming your way. Paint your picture on the canvas of your tomorrow. You can't grasp a vision you can't see. You will never see what could be if you don't know what it must be.

Pick up your paintbrush, and start transforming your Canvas of Tomorrow.